# ENGINEER

© 2024 Julie Dascoli

All rights reserved. No part of this book may be reproduced or transmitted in any form or by any means, electronic or mechanical, including photocopying, recording or by any information storage and retrieval system, without prior permission in writing from the publisher.

Published in 2024 by Amba Press, Melbourne, Australia.
www.ambapress.com.au

Previously published in 2015 by Hawker Brownlow Education.
This edition replaces all previous editions.

ISBN: 9781923116924 (pbk)
ISBN: 9781923116931 (ebk)

A catalogue record for this book is available from the National Library of Australia.

# ENGINEER

Written by Julie Dascoli

Photography by Laura Dascoli

Dear Reader,

Welcome to this volume of the *Real People Real Careers* series. I hope you'll enjoy learning all about Donna and her work as an aircraft maintenance engineer.

Before you read on, I'd like to say a few thank-yous to the people who helped to make this book possible.

Firstly, thank you to Laura Dascoli, who took the photographs you see in the book, and to Donna Dascoli, who provided initial editing and computer support services.

Secondly, my thanks to the staff and students in Years 4, 5 and 6 of the Mossgiel Park Primary School class of 2015 for their unwavering help and support.

And finally, I'm doubly grateful to Donna, who generously gave up her time to help others learn about her profession – and to show them all the ways in which her job rules!

Happy reading!

Julie Dascoli

# ENGINEER

My name is Donna and I'm a Licenced Aircraft Maintenance Engineer, otherwise known as a LAME (pronounced LAY-MI).

I went to a local high school and took subjects like maths, physics and chemistry.

When I left school after Year 12, I went to university in Queensland. I enrolled in a business degree for people who want to work in the **hospitality industry**.

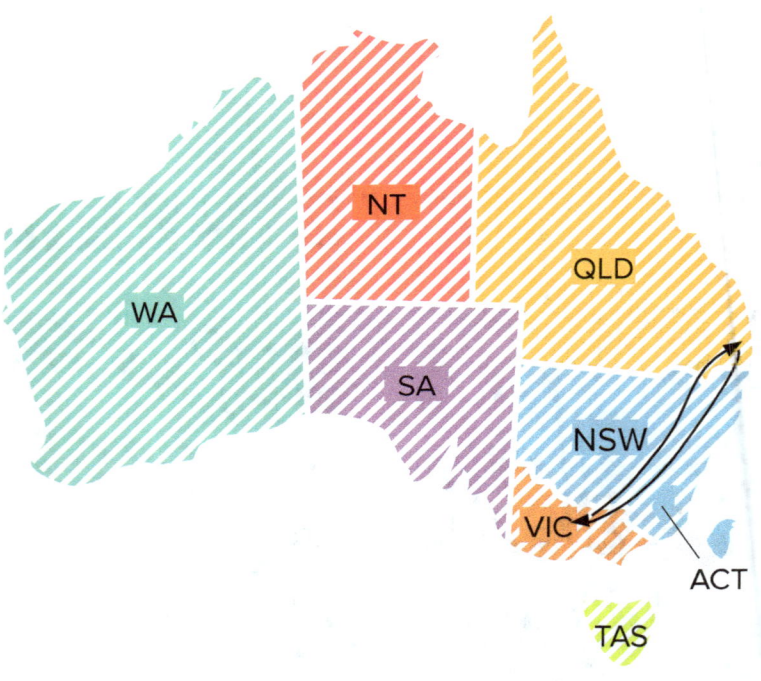

I didn't like it one bit! It wasn't for me, so I decided to come back to Melbourne to pursue my original passion to be a pilot.

I went to a small local airport in Melbourne to find out what was involved in becoming a pilot. I gathered a lot of information to take home and read, but I was very disappointed to learn that the cost was going to be astronomical! I needed to talk to my parents and work out what I should do.

While I was in the flying school's office, I saw an **advertisement** for a **trade assistant**, which is a person who helps a qualified tradesperson to do their job.

I decided to apply for the job, as it would allow me to work around aeroplanes – and you never know what opportunities could arise in the future. The **receptionist** said that I could speak to the **chief engineer** straight away, and I was given an **interview** on the spot.

The **chief engineer** asked me a lot of questions about me and my schooling. He also explained what would be expected of me if I got the job. He told me I was likely to get dirty, but I assured him that a bit of grease wouldn't worry me.

**ENGINEER**

I waited for seven long days with no news, but finally I received a phone call to say that I could have the job! I started my new job the following week.

First, I began to learn about the **hangar** and all the equipment and tools I would need to use. My supervisor taught me how to fix the aeroplanes, and I slowly got better and better at it.

After a few months, my position as a **trade assistant** turned into an **apprenticeship**. This meant that I had to start going to **TAFE**, which is a school for tradespeople where they learn all the technical skills they need to know to do their jobs and obtain **qualifications**.

I attended a **TAFE** that was over two hours away from my home. I stayed there for two weeks at a time, and during these periods I went to school every day.

There was accommodation at my **TAFE** in the form of on-campus units for the students to stay in. The company I work for paid for my accommodation.

I studied very hard, and we had exams at the end of every week. Sometimes this meant that there was no time to go out with my friends, but I tried to find a balance.

> I decided to apply for the job, as it would allow me to work around aeroplanes —
> and you never know what opportunities could arise in the future.

I went to **TAFE** for three of the four years of my **apprenticeship**. I got really good marks, so all my hard work paid off, and in my final year at **TAFE** I won the Apprentice of the Year award. I was really proud of myself.

Four years went past very quickly, and before I knew it I was a fully qualified AME, or Aircraft Maintenance Engineer.

Over the next 18 months, I did more study at home and in my office at work. This time, my goal was to complete a number of exams that would enable me to gain an engineering licence. This licence allows me to work unsupervised, and it means that I can sign all of the paperwork and legal documents for each aircraft I repair so that it can return to the air.

I am now a LAME: a Licenced Aircraft Maintenance Engineer.

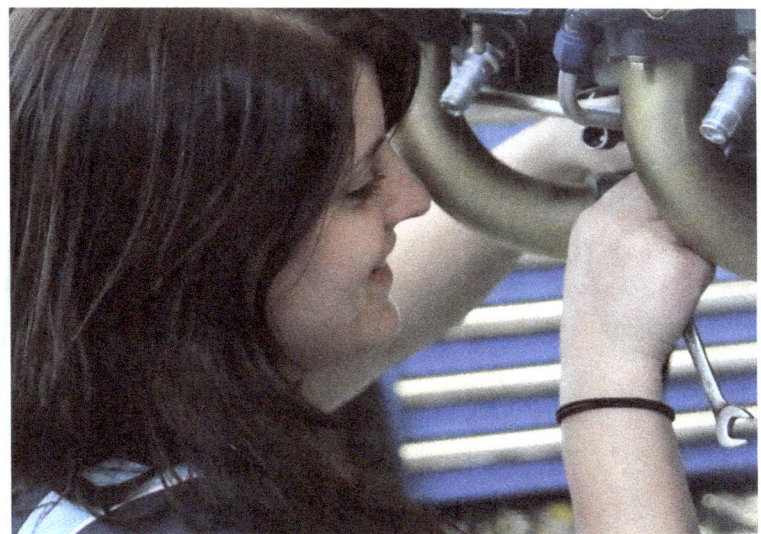

## Tasks I perform every day

- I inspect the airframe structures, including the wings, tail and **fuselage** of the aircraft.
- I also perform maintenance and repairs on the engine and its **components** as well as propellers, fuel systems, flight controls and hydraulic systems.
- It's my job to order parts and **components** when I need them to repair the aircraft.
- One of my important responsibilities is to inspect flight-control cables and pulleys to make sure they are in good condition and move freely.
- To create a safe workplace, I keep the **hangar** clean and make sure to take care of my tools.
- I also maintain aircraft logbooks in accordance with **regulations** set by **CASA**, the Civil Aviation Safety Authority.
- When maintenance is complete, I 'run up' the aircraft. This means that I start the plane, drive it onto the tarmac and check the gauges to make sure that the engine is running properly.
- I test-fly the planes when I need to, but only because I have a pilot licence. Usually an engineer would have to accompany a licenced pilot on the test flight.

## Interesting facts about my job

- I work eight hours a day.
- I get an hour-long break for my lunch.
- My favourite task is rebuilding engines.
- My least favourite task is cleaning up.
- The flying school for which I work has a fleet of approximately 14 aircraft.
- In total, we maintain around 25 aircraft.
- My dream job would be to fly for the Royal Flying Doctor Service.

**ENGINEER**

## What I wear to work

When I go to work each day, I wear a uniform. It consists of a polo shirt with the logo of the company I work for, strong and comfortable work pants, and steelcap boots. When I use machinery or power tools, I make sure my hair is tied up so that it doesn't get caught.

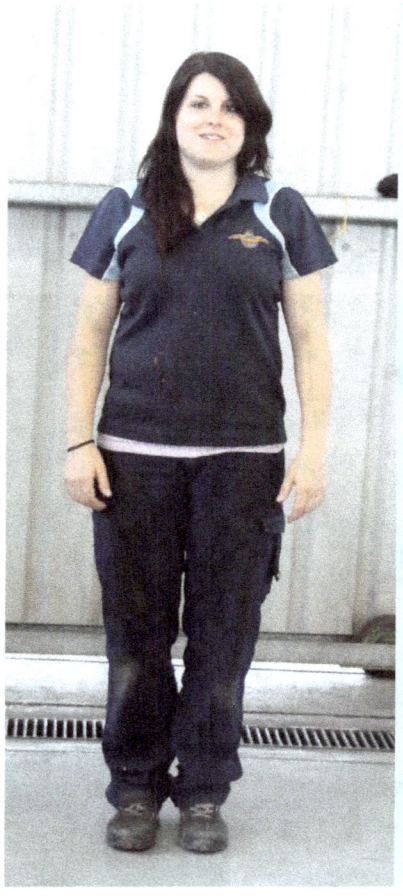

I wear a uniform. It consists of a polo shirt with the logo of the company I work for, strong and comfortable work pants, and steelcap boots.

Certain jobs require me to wear safety glasses to protect my eyes, and I wear a **respirator** when I'm painting. I also use earplugs in my ears, as the airport is very noisy.

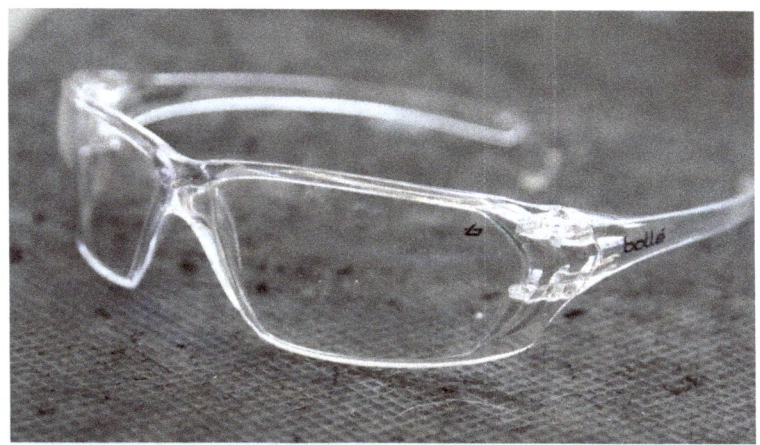

**safety glasses**

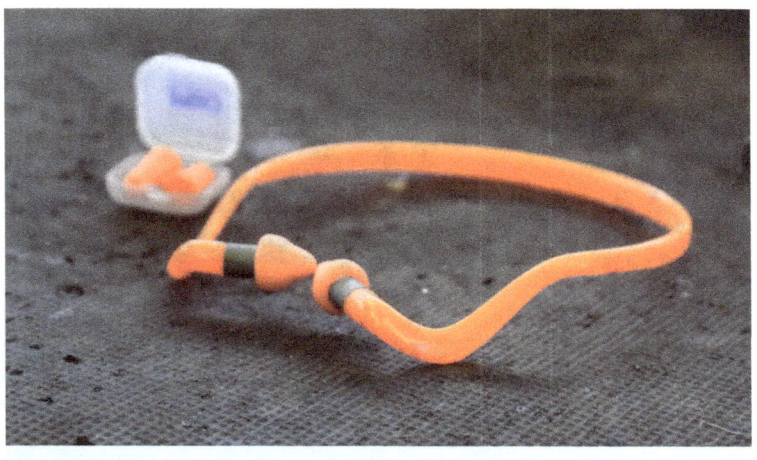

**earplugs**

**respirator**

I wear a security pass called an Aviation Security Identification Card (ASIC) on a lanyard around my neck. For security reasons, no unauthorised people are allowed to be in the airport where I work, so I must wear the pass at all times.

## Related occupations

- → avionics engineer
- → parts interpreter and distributor
- → propeller specialists
- → engine specialists
- → aviation welders
- → helicopter engineer
- → flight engineer

 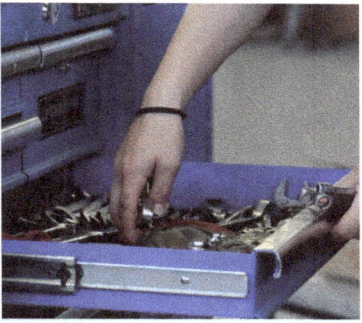

**my toolbox**

For security reasons, no unauthorised people are allowed to be in the airport where I work.

inside the hangar

keeping paperwork up to date

## Postscript

Donna has now been to America and obtained her commercial pilot licence there. She has an Australian commercial pilot licence too.

Donna won major and minor **scholarships** from a women pilots' association to assist with the cost of flying lessons. She also received an award from **CASA**, the governing body of aviation in Australia, which helped her to purchase tools for engineering. These **scholarships** have helped her immensely.

She is currently working for a well-known company in Queensland, where she works in the **hangar** doing maintenance two days per week and takes passengers on recreational flights around the islands off the coast of Central Queensland three days a week.

**twin-engine aircraft**

**instrument panel**

Donna also owns her own little single-engine plane, a Cessna 152. It is a two-seater and is mainly used for training student pilots, but she likes to go flying in it whenever she can.

**Donna's Cessna 152**

## Glossary

| | |
|---|---|
| **Advertisement** | A public notice or announcement that lets people know about a product, event, service or job vacancy. *When Donna visited the flying school, she saw a written **advertisement** stating that the school was looking for a **trade assistant**.* |
| **Apprenticeship** | A type of training that combines on-the-job work with TAFE studies over a period of three or four years. Upon the completion of an **apprenticeship**, the apprentice becomes a qualified tradesperson. *Donna did a four-year **apprenticeship** in order to earn a **qualification**.* |
| **CASA** | The Civil Aviation Safety Authority. This is the Australian government organisation that sets all the laws in aviation and makes sure that everyone follows them. *When Donna repairs planes, she makes sure to abide by the **regulations** set by **CASA**.* |
| **Chief engineer** | The person in charge of the **hangar** as well as the activities within it and the people working there. *The **chief engineer** warned Donna that she might get dirty while working as a **trade assistant**.* |
| **Component** | A part that, when put together with other parts, will create a larger item. *An aeroplane is made up of many **components**.* |

**Fuselage** — The central body portion of an aircraft that holds the crew, passengers and cargo. *Part of Donna's job is to repair aeroplane **fuselages**.*

**Hangar** — The large shed where aeroplanes are housed and maintained. *When Donna fixes aeroplanes, she does so in the **hangar**.*

**Hospitality industry** — The industry that encompasses tourism- and leisure-related services, such as restaurants, bars, hotels and so on. *Partway through her **qualification**, Donna decided that the **hospitality industry** was not for her.*

**Interview** — The process in which an employer who wants to hire a new staff member meets with a person who has applied for the job. The employer asks questions of the applicant, and the applicant can also ask questions to work out if they are the best person for the job. *Donna had an **interview** with the **chief engineer** at a local airport to see if she would be the best person for the job.*

**Qualification** — The certificate, diploma or degree that proves you have completed training in a particular field. *Donna completed a **TAFE apprenticeship** to obtain a LAME **qualification** and a flying-school course to obtain a pilot **qualification**.*

**Receptionist** An office worker who answers phones, greets people when they enter the office and answers questions in order to assist clients. *The **receptionist** was the first person Donna spoke to at the flying school.*

**Regulation** A law or rule that must be followed to guarantee that everything runs smoothly, safely and fairly. *When Donna is fixing or flying aeroplanes, everything she does must be in compliance with the **regulations** set out by **CASA**.*

**Respirator** A breathing apparatus that covers your nose and mouth to filter out harmful chemicals in the air, stopping them from entering your lungs. *For safety reasons, Donna wears a **respirator** when she paints the aeroplanes.*

**Scholarship** An award of financial assistance that is given to a student to further their education. *Donna won a **scholarship** from **CASA** that she used to pay for tools to assist with her engineering **qualification**.*

**TAFE** A vocational school where people can learn the technical skills they need to do their jobs and earn a certificate or diploma. *Donna's **TAFE** was more than two hours away from her home.*

**Trade assistant** The person who assists a qualified tradesperson with their work. *Donna wasn't sure what she wanted to do as a job until she saw an **advertisement** seeking a **trade assistant**.*

## Other titles in this series

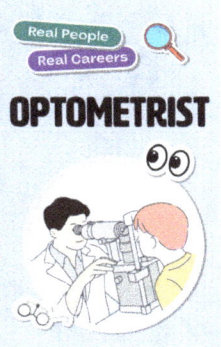

www.ingramcontent.com/pod-product-compliance
Lightning Source LLC
Chambersburg PA
CBHW070343120526
44590CB00017B/2996